AF463749

A Man Under Authority

Doug M^c^Naught

Copyright © Bekasume Books 2008. All rights reserved. No part of this book may be used or reproduced in manner whatsoever without the written permission of the publisher, except in the case of brief quotations in articles and reviews.

Contact bekasume.books@optusnet.com.au

ISBN: 978-1-4092-0472-5

Contents

Preface

I have long been a believer of complete obedience in our Christian lives so this topic is dear to my heart. After all the Lord told His disciples that anyone who wants to follow Him should deny themselves and take up their crosses; and He gave the great example of self denial in His own life.

I offer these thoughts for the benefit of all. I do not claim to be an expert or one who has achieved total obedience. These words are as much for me as they are for anyone else.

I apologize to any person who may say that I have used their ides. I gladly offer priority to anyone who wants to claim it. I must point out, however, that it is the same Holy Spirit who teaches us about our Lord Jesus Christ, the same yesterday, today and forever.

Acknowledgments

I would like to thank my wife Jenny for supporting me in so many ways as I have taken the time to prepare and write this book.

I would also like to thank Glenys Lobb for her valuable help in typing the original manuscript.

All Bible quotations are taken from the *New American Standard Bible: 1995 update*. 1995. LaHabra, CA: The Lockman Foundation (unless otherwise stated).

A Man Under Authority

"For I also am a man under authority, with soldiers under me; and I say to this one, 'Go!' and he goes, and to another, 'Come!' and he comes, and to my slave, 'Do this!' and he does it."

Matthew 8:9

I recently read a book entitled 'The Lazy Man's Way to Riches' written by a millionaire called Joe Karbo[1]. The philosophy is one that prevails in our society; there are many who spend large sums each

---

[1] Karbo, Joe *The Lazy Man's Way to Riches*, Self Published, Sunset Beach, California, 1973.

year in the hope of winning some large prize in a lottery or some other form of gambling.

Many people scan the papers eagerly each week and read the results of the latest 'draw'. They live their lives in the constant hope that they will strike it rich.

We read many stories of those who become overnight successes in show business of some other field, and these stories are read eagerly by thousands who long to emulate their path to riches.

Many people who achieve wealth or success have had to work very hard for their success, and most people who work very hard don't become rich. The people who do achieve wealth usually spend some time as poor people with very little money and experience hardship. These same people continued to work hard under trying conditions and eventually their persistence and hard work was rewarded.

There are many Christians who have allowed this philosophy to pervade their Christian outlook. They have sought to become spiritual giants overnight. They hope to lead the church to new heights but do not want to spend the many hard hours needed to grow and mature in their faith. They want the rewards without making the sacrifices.

Christians are called to a life of service. We follow the One who was obedient, even to death, a painful and shameful death. If we would walk the road of service that our Saviour seeks of us, we must learn the lessons of the centurion in Matthew 8: 5-13.

The main character in this story is the centurion. A centurion was generally an extremely capable soldier who had worked his way up through the ranks. His career began at the bottom. He had known many hardships and had performed many tasks given to him. This man had spent many cold, dark nights in the rain watching the enemy. He understood that the path of obedience was often hard and thankless. This man literally knew the meaning of the words 'I am a man under authority.'

The word used for 'servant' here is 'pais'; it can also mean an attendant or child. This servant was probably a comrade of long standing. Perhaps the man had been with the centurion on many campaigns and shared many difficult times.

The man was paralysed but there is no indication in the text of the nature of his paralysis. The problem, however, was serious; the servant was suffering. The word used for 'fearfully tormented' can also mean 'torture'. This centurion was going through a time of deep distress. His servant and, probably, his dear friend was suffering considerably. His pain was extreme and he was unable to move. This factor is important to consider because we often feel that we can relax and let down our guard when we are suffering or going through times of extreme stress.

As we look at the Saviour it is hard not to be moved by the love that he had for humanity. The gracious words 'I will come and heal him.' These words echo throughout the ages. Every sinner must gasp with joy and gratitude as he hears those words for himself. The blessed Saviour knew the need; He understood the hardship and He immediately responded in the best way possible. What a wonderful

Saviour we have! If we keep Him constantly in our minds we will be safe, even in the times of greatest trial. His love can only draw out gratitude and worship from our hearts. We will have to exclaim with wonder 'Great is the Lord" and we will fall at His feet and worship.

The centurion had already grasped something of the awesome power of the Lord. 'Just say the word!' what majesty, what authority, all He has to do is say the word and our deepest needs are met. This was the one who spoke in times past and brought the worlds into being. He is truly a man of authority.

The words for 'authority' comes from two other words: the preposition 'ex' meaning 'out of' and the noun 'ousia' meaning 'having power or wealth'. The Lord has infinite power as he controls the universe's infinite wealth, as he owns the entire universe. Our Lord does whatever he pleases no matter what we want to say or do.

This centurion understood that fact and he knew the Lord's great authority. He is man under authority himself. He says to one soldier 'go' and he goes and to another 'come' and he comes and to his slave 'do this' and he does it'. I wonder how many Christians have such high regard for the Lord that leads to this kind of obedience. His authority is great and our response must be humble and complete.

The Lord goes on to define the meaning of faith. This centurion is commended for his faith. He has seen and been impressed by the authority of the Lord; he has realised that this authority demanded a response and has come in willing subjection. Faith is the recognition of God's authority and a subsequent absolute submission to that authority.

The Kingdom of God is open to Gentiles because we have faith in the Lord Jesus Christ, while the door is closed to many who would expect to own it by right of birth because they don't have this kind of faith. The response of the local people, in Christ's day, was 'we will not have this man to reign over us'. They had a history of the powerful God Who demands obedience but when they met Him they chose to reject Him and ignore His authority.

This story closes with a fitting climax; the centurion had seen the greatness of God and rejoiced in His authority. The love and power of our Saviour is now demonstrated: he speaks the word and the servant is healed.

We of the English speaking world have treasured our democracies and expounded our rights for many years. In our feeling of superiority we have become confused; we often choose to substitute our culture for our Christianity. So often we have chosen to respect our culture and give its precepts divine authority at the expense of true Christianity. We believe that the Church is a democracy and that the direction of the Church is controlled by the will of the people. Pseudo-Christian philosophers and militant chauvinists now debate questions of doctrine and the authority of the Word of God is replaced by the consensus of vocal lobby groups.

The Lord chose to call the Church a kingdom. The term 'kingdom' implies a king and the king must be obeyed. Perhaps the most powerful king of all was

Nebuchadnezzar, in the earthly sense. He had absolute power over his subjects and they were completely under his authority. This king had the power to kill anyone whenever he wanted to. As Christians we need to make ourselves aware of the authority of our King. All His subjects must obey His laws and do precisely as He commands. This concept of absolute authority is alien to our culture but is the cornerstone of our Christianity.

We have been glad to accept His grace and now that we are members of His kingdom we must accept His authority. The Lord of Heaven has given us the Scriptures; we must make it our business to obey. Not because there is fear but because we love Him. There is a need in the life of each and every Christian to examine every aspect of his or her life under the microscope of God's word. We must always choose to obey the ways of God ahead of our earthly wisdom or feelings of consensus.

Faith is not something we own; it is an activity within our lives. If we have faith then we obey the Lord. Our faith is exercised when we hear or read the word of God and then do His will to the last detail.

We can take encouragement, as we examine the authority of the Bible, as well. The Lord who demands absolute obedience is the Lamb that was slain. We will never know the extent of His might or authority for none can measure it. We do know the full extent of His love for we know that there is no greater love than His; He lay down His life. We can confidently obey our Lord because we are secure in His love. Would He give His life to redeem us and later lead us in a way that is not good for us?[2]

The response that should come from every Christian should be similar to that of Thomas when he saw the risen Lord, 'My Lord and my God.' Let us keep the Lord Jesus before us always. He set His face towards Jerusalem; why should we debate and argue rather than read and obey? Let us not seek to usurp His authority but submit to him. His authority is beyond dispute our response must be to obey.

---

[2] Rom 8:32

Not My Will But Thine

And He was saying, "Abba! Father! All things are possible for You; remove this cup from Me; yet not what I will, but what You will."

Mark 14:36

We must never forget one important fact; if we are Christians then we have the name of Christ in our designation. Christians were so called because they bore the name of Christ in their daily lives. His name was constantly on their lips and in their minds.

In 'A New Eusebius'[3] a quote is given from Seutonius' *Life of Claudius*. The quotation concerns the expulsion of the Jews from Rome; 'Since the Jews constantly made disturbances at the instigation of Chrestus, he expelled them from Rome.' Stevenson goes on to say that Chrestus and Christus were pronounced in much the same way.

The amazing thing about this episode is that it was recounted in AD 49; some 20 years after the Lord returned to heaven. The Lord's enemies were still angry concerning His claims of the while there were others who claimed that He had come back to life and was alive. This conviction was so real in the lives of the Christians that it seemed to an outside observer that Christ was, in fact, still alive and living among the local Jewish people. This was really true; the local Christians experienced the Risen Lord in their lives every day.

We who seek to follow the Lord should find this experience true as well. If we keep the Lord in our minds all the time then we will experience His daily presence. As we remember Him we will learn progressively to hold Him in high esteem and not forget that He is Lord as well.

We follow the Lord Jesus Christ and it is good for us to examine His life and see the principles by which he lived. The topic of this book is 'A Man Under Authority'; was this concept evident in our Saviour's life? If this is evident then it will be good for us to follow this same precept in our own lives. We can examine

---

[3] Stevenson, J (ed) *A New Eusebius, Documents illustrating the History of the Church to AD 337,* London: SPCK, 1987, page 1

this fact by reading Mark 14: 35, 36, 40, 42.

These remarkable verses are well known to many Christians. Here is a picture of our Saviour as was prophesied in Lam 1: 12. His sorrow was great and the Lord in His deep anger[4] afflicted these sorrows on him. The Lord Jesus was to be the 'Man of Sorrows' who was acquainted with grief. His sorrows were genuine and extreme. We can tell from the book of Lamentations that there was no man who suffered as much as our Lord for there is no sorrow like His sorrow. Medical experts tell us that pain is intensified when a person is under stress; the pain felt by a person dying of cancer is far greater than, say, the pain felt by a severely wounded soldier just returning from the front. The first is burnt with the anxiety of facing death while the second knows that His injuries are taking him away from the place of death. (This doesn't take away from the fact that he has been heroically wounded in his country's service.)

Crucifixion was an extreme and cruel form of death. Those who were crucified were known to curse their parents and the day they were born because they were in so much pain. The blessed Son of God felt all this pain but how it must have been intensified by the mental anguish that he felt. He cried out in agony at the rejection of His Father, who could not bear to look upon the sin that He was bearing[5]. His own people rejected him; the ones he chose and loved. His spotless soul was weighed down under the burden of our sin. The leaders of the Jews falsely

---

[4] The Lord was not angry with His own Son; He was angry with Satan and the sin that was destroying the perfect world that the Lord had made.

[5] Compare Isaiah 59: 2; Heb 9: 28

accused Him and cursed Him for blasphemy that He didn't commit. Never have so many wrong things been done to a righteous man. The Lord knew about all these things before He suffered and He was troubled while He was in the garden.

We often excuse people for behaving in an irrational way when they are experiencing extreme stress but how did our Lord react? Did His behaviour become bizarre or eccentric?

Our dear Lord prayed the prayer of a troubled man. He came to the Father and poured out all the anguish of His troubled soul. Humanly speaking, He was very close to the end of His strength. This was the prayer of a man who was weary, worn and weighed down[6]. Even in these extreme circumstances the blessed Lord took time out to praise God. He acknowledged God's authority by accepting that God can control everything. He praises God that everything is under His control. Then in that context the Lord makes His request and then willingly submits himself to the authority of God.[7]

The Lord Jesus returned to the place of prayer and placed Himself, again, completely under God's authority. First, He placed himself on the altar and then He followed the path that God has set out for Him. The Lord Jesus went from the place of submission to meet His betrayer, in spite of His earlier anguish. He was completely submitted to His Father.

---

[6] The Lord Jesus wasn't contemplating a last minute 'pull out' before He went to the cross; he was satisfying the prophecy of Isaiah 63: 5. 'I looked, and there was no one to help… so my own right arm brought salvation…"

[7] This garden experience is also a fulfilment of Isaiah 63: 1-5.

The Lord Jesus is the pioneer of our faith; He went down the path before us; He blazed the trail and set the standards that we should aspire to. The Lord Jesus was the first one to come to God as Son and say to him 'because all authority is in your hands, I willingly accept that this is my life.' Those of us who want to follow the Lord must also go down this path: the path of implicit and explicit obedience. Our faith will grow and mature in the atmosphere of willing submission, of our subjecting our wills to His. Our faith is expressed in our obedience.

The one who demands obedience from us is the one who gave His life. We read in Romans 8: 32 'He who did not spare His own Son but gave Him up for us all, will not give us all things with Him?' This should be the motto of every Christian. What are the sacrifices of obedience when compared to His great sacrifice? If we obey Him we can be confident that He will not lead us down a path that is bad for us. His desire is to make us perfect so that we can be presented without blemish before the presence of His glory with rejoicing[8]. This is a great encouragement to the Christian. He will send us down in the way that will make us better and glorify His name.

As Christians examine the life of the Lord Jesus we should remember that His sorrow is the sorrow that we should have known but will never know. Our response should be to freely give ourselves to Him, in willing subjection to His will. The challenge to each one of us as we examine the life of our Lord is to ask ourselves the question 'what must I do?' When confronted by a love that is as great

[8] Jude 24

as His is our response has to be to pray the words of verse 36b, and pray it often.

I Cannot Come Down

So I sent messengers to them, saying, "I am doing a great work and I cannot come down. Why should the work stop while I leave it and come down to you?"

Nehemiah 6:3

In every sporting competition there is a team that could be given the title the 'easy beats'[9]. When the other teams play against this team they expect to win. It seems as though this kind of team has never learnt

[9] There was a popular music group called the EasyBeats but I am not referring to them.

how to win or they have forgotten how to win.

What is problem with a team like this? The players on this team have a problem with commitment. They lose concentration easily and lose the game as well. They don't try to take control of the game but allow their opponents to dictate the terms to them.

Christians often find themselves in this situation; they want to do well to the glory of God and live a victorious Christian life but instead they face an endless string of defeats. The problem can be laid at the door of commitment. There is a lovely story of a man who was really committed in Nehemiah 6: 2-9.

The request the three men made to Nehemiah seemed, on the surface, to be quite legitimate. The wall building exercise was going well, in spite of great opposition. Their opponents tried many different ways to stop the building of Jerusalem's wall. Now there seemed to be a break through in the dispute. 'We want to sort out a compromise that is acceptable to both sides'; these words seem to be the catch cry of our age, it was the same in Nehemiah's day. The sad thing about compromise solutions is that they often are made between groups who have no desire to compromise at all. Compromise is often seen as a stop along the way to getting my own way.

Nehemiah was a man of rare spiritual insight. He understood that if he left the work then the work would stop. This man saw right to the heart of the problem; if we leave our work for any reason then the work stops. Our job is to complete the task that we have been given. We should not set aside our job for any compromise solution and allow the work to lie idle.

Every Christian needs to learn the answer that Nehemiah gave: we are all involved in a great work. Perhaps we do not realise just how great the work is that we have been called to do. Maybe we should look at the price God has put on this work. The Son of God left His place of esteem, that was rightfully His, and came to live and die to pay the price of our redemption. We have not been redeemed for the sake of being redeemed. He has chosen each one of us, in spite of the fact that in ourselves there is nothing worthy, and he has a job for us to do. What a great work it must be if it cost the Lord Jesus Christ, our Saviour, His life. It is His work and, as He is great, the work is great.

Nehemiah loved Jerusalem because it was the city of God. He knew just how great the work was and he refused to leave this work for any reason. Whenever we take time away from our work it suffers and lies idle. We have each been given something to do and if we don't do our work then it will not be done properly.

The temptation faced by any Christian to abandon the work are not infrequent, in fact, we face these temptations every day of our lives. We must maintain our concentration constantly as we are faced with the temptation to leave our work. The Lord is great, His authority is absolute in all the earth and we serve Him. We need to pray for a deep understanding of His greatness and His authority and then we won't come down from our wall.

Nehemiah won the first round on points but there was no rest. The attack continued in an insidious way; he had been cupbearer to the king and was his trusted personal friend. He would have been concerned not to spoil this friendship. Nehemiah, however, was servant to a more powerful King and he was willing to pay the price to keep the work going. He was even willing to jeopardise his friendship with the king before he allowed the work to stop.

The king's cupbearer realised that he couldn't do this work in his own strength. Even though he refused to allow the work to stop he knew that he was relying on the strength of another to complete the task. He called on the God of Heaven to cause the work to prosper.

We, as Christians, who serve the Glorious King, need to understand the greatness of our work. The work is not great because we are great and it is not sustained by our own strength. It is His work and it is done in His power. The work is great but without us it may stop. Christians need to maintain their total commitment to the continuation of the work. There are many people today who seem to be concerned about the fact that there is very little life in the Church of God. Are we willing to accept His authority in our lives? Are we willing to submit our every desire and ambition to His great work? It is His work and it is great but we can only do the work as we accept His authority and rely on His power.

The incentive to continue the work can be found as we look at the Lord Jesus Christ. We know how great he is for there is no love that is greater than His love. His face was set to go to Jerusalem; he understood that if he left His work it would soon stop. Our Saviour was committed to saving others and so he was unable to save himself. How great is our Saviour and how great is His love? Can we flag in our zeal when we are confronted by love as great as this?

Christians are often willing to take time out from the work to debate. We like to have long arguments and cite a multitude of earthly authorities concerning the essentials of our faith. We forget, however, that while we debate the great work is lying idle. We are responsible to obey. He is responsible to tell us what to do and where to go. The Lord has told us what to do and we must seek to do it.

Let us daily take up the great work, where we are, and refuse to let the work cease while we take time out for civilian pursuits.

I Have Learnt To Be Content

Make sure that your character is free from the love of money, being content with what you have; for He Himself has said, "I WILL NEVER DESERT YOU, NOR WILL I EVER FORSAKE YOU,"

Hebrews 13:5

Not that I speak from want, for I have learned to be content in whatever circumstances I am

Philippians 4:11

A few years ago I worked with a large American Corporation in the computer field. When I first joined I became aware of the company indoctrination program. I started as a neophyte, fresh and uninitiated and before long was heavily involved in the intricacies of time management and setting goals. Before this I didn't realise that a person has to set goals to have a worthwhile life.

I had, in my own way, made plans and followed a purpose in my life but now I had enormous power in my hands, no longer was I a mere mortal, prey to the vagaries of my environment, I was now in total control of my environment. No man could deny me my slightest wish. I was able to set this wish down as one of my goals and no one could stay my hand. No longer could any person, or even God, deflect me from my appointment with greatness; or so they expected me to believe.

I am being cynical, for even in the great world of big business there is a certain amount of the 'old boy's network' and everyone needs to have a good friend at the right time. One important thing that I learnt, however, was the fact that no one can make me angry. Other people cannot make me angry; only I can allow myself to be angry at something that another person has done.

A person who is a total failure in life can, ultimately, only blame one person as well. I fail because I do not let myself, at least, follow some plan or purpose in my life.

As Christians, there are many things that we cannot blame on other people.

If we become embittered in life we can only blame ourselves. If we grow old and bad tempered we can only blame ourselves, for we should grow more like Christ as we grow into Christian maturity. We can see a useful commandment and its application in Hebrew 13: 5 and Philippians 4: 11.

"The love of money is the root of all evil[10]" is an often misquoted proverb and a badly misunderstood statement. This evil springs from the love of money and not from the money itself. The greater the love a person has for money, the more they are inclined to compromise true virtues in life so that they can obtain more money. We do well to keep our lives free from the love of money although that can be very hard in a society dedicated to materialism.

The love of money is bred in the home of the covetous. Once we begin to covet it begins to control us. Covetousness is the child and greed is the adult that grows out of these genes. When one is motivated by greed this love overrides all compassion, human decency and drives men to dark and dangerous deeds. However, our times seem to be founded on covetousness by another name. Advertising has the basic aim of placing a hunger for something inside our minds.

The Bible is a very useful textbook for the Christian. As we read we can find the correct way for a holy and redeemed person to live. One of the amazing things about the Bible is that it gives us positive ways of combating any evil tendencies we have. We can refuse to allow the love of money to control us in two different ways. The first, negative way is to make it our goal and then keep our minds strong

---

[10] 1 Timothy 6: 10

against any thoughts that support a covetous desire. The second, positive way is to live a lifestyle incompatible with covetousness. We are told to be content. If we concentrate on all the things that we can be thankful for then contentment will grow in our minds and we will be able to defeat the love of money. This will happen even if we don't consciously fight against covetousness.

In the early part of Hebrews 13: 5 we are told that the love of money can be a way of life and it can become a character type. The converse is also true; contentment can be a way of life and become a character type.

In Matthew 25: 9 we have the statement that is often on the lips of the discontented 'perhaps there will not be enough for us and you'. If you feel that there is not going to be enough for you then you will find that contentment is an unobtainable goal. If we are content we will have a contented mind. We feel that our needs have been met and this leads to gratitude. Contentment leads to gratitude and gratitude leads to contentment. Which comes first? We can force our minds into the contented mould by finding something to give thanks for and then give thanks will our entire mind. Christians who are content are grateful to the Lord for we know that He supplies everything that we need. Christian contentment and Christian gratitude are like two sides of the same coin. This coin brings great pleasure to our Father in heaven; it is a daily offering that we can bring to him as our worship of praise and thanksgiving.

This passage gives us a good reason to be content; 'for he has said …' These words must stand out over all our Christianity. 'He has said' so many things that bring us joy and peace. He has said that He will never leave us or forsake us. The Lord from Heaven, the One who controls all things will never forsake us to the random and arbitrary gestures of a world out of control; He will never leave us to our fate. We can be confident that He is sufficient for all our needs; after all He will always be there to see our needs and He will never forsake us to the demands of these needs. We can be sure that He is sufficient because if He were not sufficient then He would have failed and if He fails then we are forsaken. The Lord Jesus gave His life for us; this is the guarantee of all our needs. Do we believe that His love is sufficient? Then we should be content!

We can read in Philippians that this contentment is not the automatic possession of every Christian. Paul had to learn to be content. Paul learned his contentment in hardship and trial; in a life of close and blessed communion with the Lord Jesus Christ. If Paul had to learn to be content then we must learn to be content as well.

The verb 'to learn', 'manthano', is associated with the noun disciple and with discipline. Paul learned to be content through discipline; this learning took time and effort. Christians need to know discipline and this requires effort on our part. Contentment is a discipline.

One of the characteristics of a Christian life should be the gentle cheerfulness of a grateful heart. This gentle cheerfulness will not be demonstrated amid strife and discontentment. We are all glad that we have been redeemed (if we aren't then we have to wonder if we really have been redeemed); does the full implication of this enter into our minds? The Lord Jesus gave His life for us because He wanted us for Himself. He didn't just pay the great price of our salvation to promise us an eternity of joy. He gave His life for us so that we might have an abundant life now. Would the Lord from Heaven have given His life for us so that we might be bound and sad now? Paul sums all these thoughts up in Romans 8: 31, 32 "What then shall we say to these things? If God *is* for us, who *is* against us? He who did not spare His own Son, but delivered Him over for us all, how will He not also with Him freely give us all things?" There is great comfort in these words. He is preparing us to be with himself; perfect and complete and in pursuing this goal He will not spare us any good thing.

A discontented Christian is one who despises the Lord Jesus who gave His life for us. Contentment is not just something that comes and stays. Anything that just comes is something that just goes. If contentment comes to us because of our circumstances then it is likely to go if our circumstances change. We must learn to be content in spite of our circumstances for then contentment will stay even though our circumstances change. We must bring our minds into a state of contentment for He has said that He will not fail us or forsake us and if He is our helper then who can harm us?

Whether It Is Good Or Evil We Will Obey

"Whether it is pleasant or unpleasant, we will listen to the voice of the LORD our God to whom we are sending you, so that it may go well with us when we listen to the voice of the LORD our God.

Jeremiah 42:6

When I was five years old I left home. Look at any five year old child and imagine what it would be like for them to be sent away from their parents. I could not possibly imagine sending any of my four children away from home when they were five. I used to look at my children when they were that age and weep when I though about having to send them away from home. At that age they are so young and vulnerable.

My parents were missionaries in India and had the unbelievable task of deciding to send four or five year old children away to boarding school four times. They had to determine the best course of action when the long term was considered. As a child I often used to long for my parents to come and take me away from that place so that I could be with them. I knew, later, that they would weep after they had left us at that place and driven a few hundred yards down the road.

Missionaries have to face many heart breaking decisions as far as their families are concerned. They also have to face difficult decisions when they consider the long term effects of these decisions on their children's lives. Hard decisions face every Christian in their daily lives. We are frequently faced with the prospect of obeying God even though it seems to be foolish in terms of earthly wisdom.

Many times in the Scriptures people were faced with the choice of immediate personal benefit or obedience. Many people chose immediate personal benefit while others chose obedience.

We must stress that the pathway of obedience is not always detrimental to one's career or personal advancement. However, when the short term is considered, it often looks as though the pathway of obedience will be detrimental.

There is a wonderful story in the book of Jeremiah of some people and their reaction to this question. Read Jeremiah 43: 1-6.

This passage will be better understood if we take time to examine the context. Sometimes the full implications of Scriptural lessons are missed if we don't carefully consider the context.

Jeremiah lived during the last turbulent years of the kingdom of Judah. This whole story is a long, sad chronicle of disobedience and the tendency towards disobedience. The people belonged to God; they had been given many wonderful things by God, they ruled by God's chosen king but yet they preferred the ways of the neighbouring nations.

Jehoiachin had been king for three months and then he surrendered to the Babylonians who were besieging the city. He was taken away to Babylon where he spent the rest of his life in exile as the recognised king of Judah.

Zedekiah, his uncle, was appointed as caretaker ruler by the Babylonian king. These Babylonian rulers went away and left Zedekiah to rule the people and pay their taxes. The Lord told Judah that they should obey their new overlords and to be subject to their authority. Zedekiah remained true to the Lord for ten years and then he surrendered to the pressure of a pro-Egyptian faction. Zedekiah withheld the tribute he was due to pay to the Babylonians on behalf of Judah and Jerusalem. The Babylonians came and besieged the city again for one and a half years, punctuated by a brief period when they went away and defeated the Egyptians. When the people finally surrendered Jerusalem was substantially burnt and Judah lost its status as a vassal kingdom. A Babylonian public servant now ruled Judah as a Babylonian province.

Five years later the Babylonian governor was murdered in a palace revolt. At this stage some of the Jews decided to flee to Egypt and they wanted to take Jeremiah with them.

The leaders of the remnant who wanted to flee came to Jeremiah and asked him to ask the Lord for direction. Jeremiah had faithfully served the Lord for many years and they knew that he would be able to hear this message.

Jeremiah told the people that he was not in the habit of massaging their ears. So often the people had listened to the prophets who had a message of their own rather than the message from God. These prophets always told the people whatever they wanted to hear. Jeremiah told these people that he wasn't interested in protecting their fragile egos or their pride. He promised to go the Lord and tell them the message without any compromise.

After many years of wilful disobedience these people were finally broken before the Lord. They had followed their own desires for many years and all they experienced was hardship and defeat. They had finally come to realise that the way to real security and peace could only be found in obeying the Lord.

These people said that they would obey the voice of the Lord even if obedience seemed to go against their own better judgment. Some versions of the Bible, like the one quoted at the beginning of this chapter, use the words 'favourable' or 'unfavourable' here but the meaning of the words is much stronger than just favourable or unfavourable[11]. Paul went back to Jerusalem even though he knew that he was going to be imprisoned; imprisonment is not merely unfavourable. The Lord Jesus set His face to go to Jerusalem knowing that he would be falsely accused and crucified. If we are only willing to accept minor inconvenience as the price of obedience we will certainly become disillusioned.

These people had reached the position where they understood that obedience was the only way. They had to obey the Lord. At last these people knew that they would be in a good position as long as they obeyed under every circumstance

The church today seems to have lost this brokenness of spirit that is so essential when we want to serve the Lord. Some of our leaders have usurped the authority of the Scriptures and have set themselves up as dividers of the truth. They tell the people that certain portions of the Scripture only have cultural significance and there are many things that we don't have to obey. These leaders 'lord it over' the congregation and show no humility. Many church members will not submit themselves to the authority of the God appointed leaders in the church. Many Christians have forsaken the Scriptural ideals of marriage preferring to run to and fro after the popular ideals of those who seek to lead the people into total anarchy.

The Church has become seduced by the principles laid down by Gandhi. We now prefer civil disobedience and overthrow any authority in our lives.

Anybody who wants to submit themselves to the Lord can do so with

[11] The King James Version uses the words 'good' or 'evil'.

complete confidence because we are the recipients of God's love. He gave His Son to buy our freedom and He will not bring us into bondage. One day every person will have to kneel before the Lord and acknowledge His Lordship. We have been given the opportunity to do this now; we can experience His love and know the Judge as Father. Let us learn this brokenness of spirit 'whether it is good or evil we will obey the voice of the Lord our God.'

To Purpose In The Heart

But Daniel made up his mind that he would not defile himself with the king's choice food or with the wine which he drank; so he sought permission from the commander of the officials that he might not defile himself.

Daniel 1:8

When I was about three years old my parents gave me a small, spring loaded pop gun to play with. The gun broke in the middle and bent back to lard the spring and a cork, attached to a piece of string, was placed in the end of the gun. When the trigger was released the cork flew out of the end of the gun and then swung down once the limit of the string was reached.

I made up my mind that I was going to shoot a tiger. In those days, there were still hunters, men of mystique and hidden flair; there were also tigers to hunt. We lived in Bangalore and our neighbourhood was sadly deficient in tigers to hunt. In those days my family didn't allow me to use the family car so my tiger hunting expeditions were limited to family excursions.

At last the great arrived. I was to meet with my destiny and achieve immortality of sorts. My family had planned a day at the zoo. Even at that tender age, I knew that there were tigers at the zoo. I was not greatly concerned with the ethics of shooting a tiger in a cage and people were not yet concerned with wildlife and animal liberation.

I carefully laid my treasured gun in the care after I had painstakingly ensured that it was in optimum working condition. I behaved with discretion and carefully examined the other cages before I gave my attention to the tiger's cage. I examined my surroundings and carefully calculated the best approach, so that my shot would not be wasted.

My moment had arrived! I put my plan into action. I carefully approached the cage. I stepped inside the protective railing and raised my gun to the bar. The tiger noticed my approach and at the appropriate time opened his mouth and roared. I had not yet fired my gun but I was suddenly overtaken by great fear. I dropped gun right in front of the tiger café and ran for my life.

There are many of us who decide that we are going to serve the Lord with great distinction but we are like I was on that day. We plan and then put our plan into action but when we enter the furnace of hardship we leave our weapons and run wildly from the foe.

One of the outstanding men of the Old Testament was Daniel. He did not decide that he would be great, he made up his mind, purposed in his heart, as the King James Version writes, not to defile himself and then he didn't let himself be defiled. Read from Daniel 1: 3-16.

Daniel began his life in that tempestuous period of Jewish history that we considered in the last chapter. He was brought up as a devout Israelite. While he was still relatively young, Daniel was rudely taken away from his home and everything that meant security to him. He was placed in an extremely difficult situation. I wonder what our reaction would have been. I know what I would have done. I would have made up my mind to maintain a low profile. I would have said 'God has put me in these circumstances and it is my responsibility to survive so that at some later time I will still be alive and then I can serve with the wisdom I have gained from this experience.' An old proverb says: 'he who fights and runs away lives to fight another day but he who in the battle's slain will never live to fight again.'

Fortunately for us, Daniel was made of much sterner stuff. Daniel made up his mind that his first responsibility was to remain pure. He would not allow anything to happen that would make him ceremonially unclean. This great prophet of the Lord made up his mind; he resolved in his heart that no matter what happened he would not compromise on one point.

The Lord had given many Laws the Israelites so that they would know how to behave as the Lord's redeemed people. Many of their Laws concerned eating. There were special dietary Laws relating to eating meat so that they would never eat meat that contained blood. Meat also had to be prepared in a special way so that they didn't eat any fat. Meat that was not killed and prepared according to these Laws would make a person ceremonially unclean. Daniel was living in the king's precinct and had the opportunity to eat the king's food. This food, including the meat, was prepared according to Babylonian standards and not the standards defined by the Law of the Lord. The meat was probably also killed in honour of other gods. Even though he was very young, Daniel knew that eating the king's rich food would make him ceremonially unclean. This caused Daniel a problem, he solved this problem by refusing to let himself become unclean.

I think if I had been there I would have shown less integrity that Daniel. Why not just sit down and enjoy the rich food, after all the Lord has put it there for my benefit. Anyway if I starve then I will be no use to anyone. A good example of my kind of attitude is found in 2 Kings 5: 18; Naaman said he believed in God but he was still willing to go into the house of Rimmon to worship so that he could keep his job.

Daniel was more concerned with remaining true to his God. He would not eat anything that might destroy his relationship with the Lord. Daniel put the Lord before everything else.

Often in our Christian lives we feel that it is better to keep a low profile and make no waves. Daniel's first objective was to remain undefiled and in doing so any objective concerning a low profile had to be sacrificed. The rest of the narrative describes how Daniel remained true to his God. Daniel endured a great deal of hardship but he remained pure. God saw that Daniel served the Lord wholeheartedly and he honoured Daniel for this.

Daniel is one of the Old Testament prophets. Written in his prophecy are some of the great insights that we have into the times of the end. The future from Daniel's day forward is predicted precisely and concisely with almost unbelievable accuracy. God richly blessed Daniel, so much so that he talked to angels and had a deep insight into God's mind.

Great revelations only come to me who were great like Daniel. Daniel's greatness was found in his humility[12] and his refusal to be defiled. In the final analysis there are no great men or women of God there are only men and women of the great God but God allows these men and women to enjoy His greatness.

There is much defilement in the world today and sometimes it is so subtle that we accept it without question. Every Christian has a choice as to the level of

---

[12] Daniel 2: 26-28

defilements he will tolerate in his life. There is also the insidious defilement that comes when we mistake our culture for our Christianity. So often it is easier to remain true to our culture than it is to remain true to Christ.

If we want to have Christian greatness, that is, knowing the joy of belonging to the great God. If we want to see the Lord's name praised and honoured then we must make up our minds that we will not tolerate any defilement in our Christian lives.

Daniel and Joseph were two great men in the Scriptures; they both had great insights into God's mins and were able to bring His plans to men. Both of these men went out of their way to remain undefiled even at the cost of death[13] or imprisonment. Any person who seeks to remain undefiled will have a rich and fruitful knowledge of the Lord.

God calls us to remain undefiled and we need to make Daniel's resolution our own. It is possible to be defiled in thought as much as in deed. The greatest defence against defilement is to fill our minds with the Word of God and gratitude.

[13] Daniel and his friends faced death but they were saved by God's grace.

The People Who Know Their God

By smooth words he will turn to godlessness those who act wickedly toward the covenant, but the people who know their God will display strength and take action.

Daniel 11:32

It has been said that litigation has surpassed sexual activity as the pastime of the middle aged in the United States. People have become more educated and hence have become more aware of their rights. These same people have more and more leisure time and want to use it for their own personal benefit. The combination of these factors leads to the situation where people want to get as much as they can for themselves.

Christians are in a far more enviable position than any person in any country. Our 'rights' have been obtained at great cost to the Lord Jesus Christ and are secure in the fact of His resurrection.

We are sons and daughters of the King and as such have a glorious inheritance. It is good for us to search the Scriptures and discover all the things that we have been given. As we search the Scriptures we will able to fully enter in to all the benefits of our inheritance. Daniel 11: 29-32 describes some sad circumstances but there is a bright promise as well. We can be victorious and secure as we discover the full extent of our inheritance.

One of the most fascinating prophecies of Scripture is found in the eleventh chapter of Daniel. The predictions in this chapter are so precise and accurate that Daniel has been slandered by the 'liberal' scholars of our day. These men who have chosen not to believe that God knows the future and can perform miracles refuse to acknowledge that God's hand is evident in the Bible so they say that this had to be written after it happened rather than before. The Lord carefully detailed the Ptolemaic and Seleucid periods of history before they began. The, so called, 'silent years' were never really silent. The Lord wrote about them before they began.

Our Saviour called Daniel a prophet as recorded in Matthew 24: 15. It is better to trust His word and accept that Daniel was a prophet than men who have set themselves up as arbiters of God's activity. We, who know and love the Lord Jesus, cannot fail to be impressed by the greatness of our god and His absolute control over every second of time.

Daniel 11 discusses the king of the north, a member of the Seleucid dynasty, and the king of the south, a member of the Ptolemaic dynasty. These kings change with time and their relative importance varies. The period under discussion in these chapters is the period dominated by Antiochus Epiphanes, the king of the north. He called himself Epiphanes meaning magnificent and had an enormous amount of respect for himself. Other called him Epimanes, meaning madman.

At one point in time the Jews were glad because they thought that he had been defeated. He came in a great rage against the Jews. He hated them and, like so many since, made up his mind to destroy these people and their religion. He desecrated the Temple by setting up a statue of Jupiter Olympus and offering a sow on the altar. He associated himself with Jupiter Olympus and so, in setting up the statue, attempted to show his power over God's people. The daily sacrifice was forbidden in the Temple for some time after this.

The various factions that so divided the Jews and dominated their lives during the Lord's time were born during this period. Some of the people tried to ingratiate themselves with the new ruler. The compromised their religion and sold their minds to Antiochus. He sold the High Priesthood to the highest bidder. These people became the Sadducees of the Lord's day. Some Jews became rigid and unbending in their dealings with anything that came from the outside. They sought to codify their religion and bind it tightly with rules and regulations.

Even in this time of extreme cruelty when a brutal madman tried to destroy God's people there were some who remained true to the Lord and did not compromise. The Jewish religion and the Lord's people survived this time of hardship and are still alive and strong now when very few people have even heard of Antiochus Epiphanes.

The secret of their victory was the fact that they knew their God. People who know their God can display strength and take action, even in times of absolute despair and defeat. Antiochus was a vicious and twisted madman. He hated the Jews and there was no act of sadism or brutality that he did not use in order to destroy God's people.

We are living in a day when there is even greater pressure to destroy our religion. Ephesians 6: 12 tells us about our enemy; he is no less determined to destroy the people who love the Lord and he is eager to use every device to destroy the true religion. We do not battle against flesh and blood but against the principalities and powers, against the world rulers of this present darkness, against the spiritual host of wickedness in the heavenly places.

Our enemy is engaged in a mortal struggle and he is determined to win and there is no trick or device that he will not use in order to bring about our defeat. Our enemy is experienced and cunning and, as mere mortals, we will find it impossible to resist him.

We are locked in this deadly struggle and there is only one defence; we must know our God. We need to remember that He is the One who paid the price of our redemption and He is sufficient for all our needs even our most extreme needs in the deadly conflict. He is our king and we must obey Him.

The people who know their God are able to display strength, the trial of their faith will not break them but it will purify them for His glory. Every soldier needs a good defence. Not even the greatest swordsman can be useful if he cannot defend himself for he will soon be dead and his skill will be useless. The people who know their God have a sure defence and will not fall even in the times of greatest trial. We should pray for the defence of knowing our God.

The people who know their God can also take action. People with a good defence can only keep their present position; if we cannot win a war then we will eventually lose that war. Not only do we need to defend ourselves but we also need to take action. We, who know our God, are able to take the offensive. We can venture into the strongholds of darkness and fight against its insidious powers. We, who know our God, can go out and claim new ground and victories of faith for the glory of our God.

It is the responsibility of every Christian to know their God. We can learn to know our God in only one way; we know Him through prayer and Bible study and daily application of our faith. Christians who are mature also have the responsibility of teaching those who are not so mature.

In Quietness And In Confidence

For thus the Lord GOD, the Holy One of Israel, has said, "In repentance and rest you will be saved, In quietness and trust[14] *(confidence) is your strength." But you were not willing,*

Isaiah 30:15

One of the real growth industries in from the late seventies till today is the success industry. Fast talking men and women collect five figure sums of money from unsuspecting people to make them into millionaires. Of course the only people who become millionaires are those who run the courses.

Success and successful have been carefully analysed and dissected and every

[14] The King James Version uses the word confidence here.

aspect of their lives have been subjected to close scrutiny. There are many lists available of the dogged determination and aggression needed by those who want to succeed. Some of the factors that have been enumerated include setting goals and objectives, dedication lateral thinking and so on.

One thing that is basic to this list but not often discussed in confidence; a person who is confident will succeed where another person will probably stumble and fall. Confidence is at the heart of success.

During times when the economy is 'bad' business men at sales conventions will moan about lack of confidence in the market place. When there is no confidence the people in the market place will not invest the big dollars that make the eyes of sales managers shine.

Confidence is a vitally important aspect of our Christianity. If we are not confident in our Lord then we will not effectively use His power in our daily lives. Isaiah 30: 15 has something to say about this important aspect of our Christian walk.

The thirtieth chapter of Isaiah describes the sad story of the Israelites as they try to fail. The set out to make an alliance with Egypt; they are afraid of other enemies who may attack them so they want to have a strong friend. The Lord's people make no real attempt to consult the Lord or lay their concerns at His feet. They were faced with a problem; they probably had some sort of think tank and then after assessing the threat laid out possible scenarios. The final objective was maintenance of their security and the solution was to buy protection. Egypt was the strongest nation in the immediate area so they decided to buy their protection from them.

Isaiah brought this message; you will not find any protection from Egypt. These Egyptians will not be worthwhile friends; Israel belongs to the Lord and He is their real Friend. If the Lord is Israel's real Friend then they should rely on him and not some other broken down friend.

The Lord asked Isaiah to write His message down on a tablet. This message is written down like a contract and there can be no future argument about the exact wording. The Lord wanted to say something to His people and the message is clear and unambiguous. Isaiah wrote the message down so that the people can read the Lord's words in the future and they will know then that He was right.

The Lord clearly condemns His people for their disobedience and infidelity. They were wrong and the Lord is angry with them so He tells them that they are wrong. Israel's God chides them for their rebellion; they refuse to listen to His instructions.

Even as the Lord condemns His people He gives abundant evidence of His grace. He explains to His people that they can be reconciled. There can be no reconciliation without forgiveness but he is the forgiving God. God gives His people the correct scenario, they are told the best plan, now they know the way that is really safe.

These people can only find lasting and absolute security in returning to the Lord. They are His people; they have been told many times how to conduct themselves as the Lord's people. Now they must return to His ways and follow them without question. Israel is told that they need to rest in the Lord's promises and trust in His ability to keep His word. The only way to show this confidence is by obeying the Lord in every detail of their lives.

Abraham's descendants will only find their salvation in obedience and the Lord's faithfulness in keeping His word. Their strength is quietness and trust.

'Quietness' is a word that means 'rest', 'stillness' or 'repose'. There is no strength is anxiety or running around; the people need to cast themselves full on the Lord and rely completely on His ability.

'Confidence' or 'trust' is derived from a word meaning 'safety' or 'refuge'; the word means 'safety' or 'security'. The Lord is in complete control of every femtosecond[15] and it is not His will for His people to know defeat or despair, unless they choose to reject His protection. We need to trust in the safety of His love and power all day every day.

The last word of this phrase is 'strength'. 'Strength' is derived from a word meaning 'powerful' and can also mean 'victory' or 'mastery'. To be in the best position, the position of power does not come from trickery or personal excellence; it comes from quietness and trust.

---

[15] In 1999 Ahmed H. Zewail was awarded the Nobel Prize for Chemistry; he used a laser camera that was photographing every femtosecond (10^{-15} seconds)

The vital spark that a Christian needs to succeed is confidence. We need to be sure of our position and confident that we know the best way. So often we become apologisers and try to explain our beliefs in a way that is beyond the criticisms of the world. We do not take and aggressive stand because we have the best way; we tend to be defensive as though we are not sure of our ground. Do we truly believe all that the Lord has told us? Do we say with joy and authority that we are free or do we try to water down this wonderful truth with some insipid explanation? Christians are on the side of right, truth and might; do we behave with the confidence that this should inspire or are we frightened? We are called to be witnesses and we have no brief to be apologisers.

The confidence we have must come from the Lord or it will be false confidence. If we are not confident in our strength or our own ability then we are weak but the Lord chooses the weak and the foolish. Elijah needed to be quiet and free from anxiety before he heard the still small voice of the Lord. We must take care to free ourselves from all anxiety, choosing rather to rest in His strength and to trust in His might.

It is beautiful to remember that the Lord does not only give us commands, He gives us promises as well. As we rely on Him more and more and less on ourselves or what we can obtain; we will gain a sense of sweet repose and we will have to strength to be victorious.

Each Christian needs to learn that freedom from anxiety is not dependent on our circumstances but on victory in our minds. We need to discipline our minds to rest in the strength of the Lord and to be confident in His ability. As we trust in His might and rest in His security we will know His victory for His glory and our joy.

We Cannot Stop Speaking

'for we cannot stop speaking about what we have seen and heard.'

Acts 4:20

Everybody has outstanding moments in their lives, the memories of which remain for years. We often find ourselves remembering the joy of these moments with real pleasure at the most unexpected times.

One moment that I still remember after many years was the first goal I scored as a grade hockey player. I can remember all the details clearly. The closest I got to scoring before that was earning a penalty and having someone else convert the goal.

I was playing on the left wing and was given a cross ball from the right half. I raced around the opposing halves and collected the ball; now there were three players, including the goal keeper for me to beat before I could score a goal.

In those days my greatest sporting asset was my speed so I used my speed to run outside the first back and stay in front of any cover defence running back to intercept my raid. I brought the ball across the front of the other back and into the circle to the left of the goal. The goalkeeper stood close to the near post and came out to decrease my angle. He tried to bluff me into shooting where he wanted me to shoot. I squeezed the ball between the goalkeeper's waist and the near post. I shot high enough to miss his pads and low enough to evade his hands. I can still remember the supporters cheering behind the goal and the feeling of ecstasy that I had. The goal was important to me for another reason because it was the winning goal.

Another things that I clearly remember was my reaction at work on the following Monday. I was the first teacher to arrive in the staff room but I didn't waste any time wondering how I could engineer the conversation so that I could casually slip the story of my goal in at the appropriate moment. I certainly didn't go home that night disappointed that I had been unable to share my great news with my colleagues. As each member of the staff came to work I told them my news straight away.

The point of this story is quite simple; we are quick to let others know about things that are significant in our estimation but things that are not so significant are often left in our minds without being shared.

Many Christians seem to be afraid to share their Christianity, they like to hide it in some quite corner of their hearts and leave it there undisturbed.

The story that concludes in Acts 4: 18-20 describes quite a different attitude. Peter and John went together to the Temple to pray. The early disciples loved to pray and spent a lot of time in prayer as the Lord Himself had done.

While they were in the Temple; they saw a man being carried to the Temple to beg for alms. Peter stopped and looked at the man; his heart must have leapt in anticipation. How many times had this man asked for money from worshippers? How many times had people rushed past without stopping to look choosing to pretend they had not seen him so that they would not have to say 'no'? Not many people would stop and look and then walk away. This hungry man, perhaps, was already tasting his next meal.

Then the sudden lurch of disappointment; 'Look mate, I don't have any silver or gold.' Oh no, why are you tormenting me; what a cruel joke to stop and tease like that. I suppose you will have a good laugh when get together with your mates later. But wait a minute, he is still speaking. 'I do have something to give you.' Wow, perhaps this wasn't such a bad joke after all. 'In the name of Jesus Christ, get up and walk.' His words had such authority, can I dare to disobey? No I can't disobey the words, what power there seems to be in that name. But wait a minute; I can't walk but I can't disobey. Oh well, here goes nothing. So far so good; I'm standing up; how does one walk, I wonder? One foot out in front and now the other; I am walking! Praise the Lord; I can't stop myself from dancing.

The man started walking; he was so excited that he had to dance and praise the Lord. What a commotion; soon there was a large crowd of inquisitive worshippers straining to see what was happening. Was it the Temple guard evicting a Gentile? Perhaps there was a fight? There were two men standing together and another man was jumping around and shouting like he had won the lottery. That happy man certainly looked familiar; he was the one who used to sit, begging outside the Temple gate. What a fraud he must be.

Peter saw the crowd and he just couldn't help himself. He had just been involved the most incredible event in the history of the human race. The Man and Teacher that he respected more than any other person in the world, the One he believed to be the Messiah, was killed like a common criminal. All his dreams were shattered; but in three days he had seen this Man as the Risen Lord. The Risen Lord came to Peter and spoke to him, He knew about his sins, especially the fact that Peter had denied that he knew the Lord, and forgave them. But that wasn't all; the Lord went back to heaven and God the Holy Spirit came and filled his life. Peter was the most blessed man on earth; the Risen Lord had spoken to him, he was filled with the Holy Spirit and he couldn't stop himself from speaking about all these things. Peter knew that his sins were forgiven and he was free so he preached the gospel.

When someone starts preaching with such power it doesn't take long for Satan to organise some opposition. Peter was talking about the resurrection but that wasn't acceptable. They quickly pulled them up and accused them of some crimes and then rushed them into jail.

Peter and John went down to the jail but later they were taken to the religious rulers. These people asked them to explain their activities. The situation was difficult because these men were masters of academic and legal procedure and had learnt every device needed to confound their opponents. If Peter and John could quote from the proper authorities then maybe all would be forgiven.

Peter was just a compulsive preacher, he couldn't help himself. Here he stood and over there was another captive audience. He didn't bother to quote authorities; Peter just started to preach the gospel. He was an evangelist and he had the good news to proclaim. He wasn't concerned about the status of these men; he knew that they were sinners and were eligible for salvation.

The rulers didn't really have much of a case to convict the apostles with any severe or capital offence. The man who couldn't walk for all those years was walking around now; it would be hard for them to quietly dispose of this man because too many people had seen the miracle. There was other strong evidence; Peter himself, he preached with such power that they could not explain it away with some technical legal argument.

The rulers issued a stiff reprimand to Peter and John. They were told that they must never preach in that name, the name of the Lord Jesus Christ. It was apparent that the power of the Holy Spirit was available to Peter but they tried to stop the process that they had already tried to stop before at Calvary.

Peter posed a question to his judges in answer. Each of us has to answer this question in our hearts today. 'What is right in God's sight; to listen to and obey man or God?' Peter immediately told the rulers his answer; 'it doesn't matter how you answer this question, there is nothing on earth that can stop me from preaching about the marvellous things that have happened in my life.'

Peter and John were so filled with the greatness of their experience that they couldn't keep quiet about it. This experience had been so wonderful and significant in the lives that they had to tell everyone that they met about it. We, Christians today, are often so constrained through real and other reasons not to speak about our salvation.

I believe that this constraint is born in the fact that we are not fully convinced of the greatness of our experience. Is our Christianity the most significant thing in our lives? Do we really rejoice in our salvation? Is this something that we appreciate above everything else? Perhaps our Christianity is just another part of our mundane existence.

Christians often seem to show that their Christian experience is just a 'valley of the shadow of death' experience rather than a 'green pastures and still waters' experience. The Lord Jesus told His followers 'Take My yoke upon you and learn from Me, for I am gentle and humble in heart, and YOU WILL FIND REST FOR YOUR SOULS. For My yoke is easy and My burden is light.'[16] If we don't completely submit to His yoke then we will not be amazed at just how light it is, we won't rejoice in its easiness.

The amazing thing about being a Christian is that it is better than any other lifestyle. We have been promised the peace of God; we will be kept and we can always know His sufficiency. These things are not just pious phrases easily flung from our mouths, they are living effective promises and they are guaranteed in the resurrection of the Lord Jesus. He is alive in heaven to make sure that we will receive everything that He has promised us.

We who live in this fearful generation of Christians need to learn the greatness and goodness of our heritage. We need to become excited about being Christians, about knowing the Risen Lord, about being filled with the Holy Spirit and then we will not be able to keep quiet. We will start to tell others just how good and how great our Lord is and how many good things that he has done for us.

---

[16] Matthew 11: 29, 30 *New American Standard Bible: 1995 update*. 1995. LaHabra, CA: The Lockman Foundation.

You Have Left Your First Love

'But I have this against you, that you have left your first love.'

Revelation 2:4

In the last few months I have heard about two amazing court cases. These cases are considered to be 'landmark decisions'; perhaps they will be discussed in laws schools but the implications for ordinary mortals are staggering indeed.

The first case concerns a man who was at one time in Australia. He was accused of many crimes associated with drugs but left the country. Eventually the police found him in another country. He was arrested by the local police and held while the Australian police prepared a case for his extradition.

When the case came to court it was found to have substance and the man was to be extradited. His lawyers found some technicality on which the man could be releases and the courts knowingly released a man who was charged with murder.

The second case involved two confidence men in the United States. These men made an agreement in relation to a swindle. One of the men had previously been involved in this swindle and the second man came from a big city and they agreed to increase the size of this crime. After a while the first man was concerned that the second man was too corrupt so he tried to back out of the agreement. The second man shot and killed the first man for breaking the deal. When the police came to the crime scene they found a tape recorder in the desk drawer. The last meeting between the two men was taped so the criminal was found guilty as the evidence was overwhelming.

The murderer was convicted but when the verdict was appealed the evidence was ruled inadmissible because the murderer had not consented to the tape being made. The victorious lawyer, when interviewed, showed no remorse for the fact that a known murderer was set free. He claimed that this case was a triumph for the rule of law.

I am not sophisticated or very wise but it seems to me that the law should support justice. Here are two cases where the law was definitely thwarted and justice became the friend of murderers. There must be something wrong with our understanding of justice when this can happen openly without the slightest murmur of dissent.

As we around at the church of God we can see certain inconsistencies that are glaringly similar. There is something missing in many churches today. We need to try and find out the point at which we left the narrow path and then we can return to the correct way.

Revelation 2: 1-7 describes the first point at which the church or an individual goes astray.

The letters to the seven churches in Asia are generally accepted by conservative scholars as being descriptive of the phases of decline of the church during her age.

Ephesus is the fist church in this section and so it describes the post apostolic age and the first step in the church's decline. The inevitable end of this decline is the Lord standing outside the church or the heart of the Christian knocking and waiting to be readmitted.

Ephesus was a very wealthy city in Asia Minor. It was a port city on the Cayster River. Ephesus was the centre of the worship of the goddess Artemis. She was the goddess of a fertility cult and the city had gained a great deal of wealth from worshipping her. Ephesus was also famous for it magic.

The seven stars represent the ministers of the gospel. These ministers are under God's protection and they are His instruments. He holds the churches and the ministers of the gospel in His hand. He is also constantly moving among them and knows if anything is wrong.

The Lord tells each church that he knows; these are comforting words for every Christian. He knows all about our hardships and trials. The Lord knew all about the hard work and patience endurance of the church at Ephesus. They resisted the lure of the false gospel and did not allow evil men to lead them astray. These men and women chose to trust in the Word of the Lord.

The times were hard but the Ephesians endured for the sake of the Lord's Name; they continued because of His character. The hardships were endured for His Name's sake. These Christians did not grow weary when life seemed to be too hard and the heavens seemed to be brass when they prayed. It is easy to grow weary but those Christians did not grow weary.

There was, however, one complaint against this church; they had left their first love. Christians, when we are converted and are growing to maturity love the Lord above all things but after many trials it is easy to leave this first love.

These Christians were called upon to look at themselves and to see the state to which they had fallen. They are encouraged t return to their first status. Do we seek the Lord wholeheartedly as we are encouraged to do in Psalm 119: 10? Perhaps we do not have this wholehearted devotion; then we should consider what we have fallen from and return to our former level of devotion.

The Lord holds the seven stars and they are under His control; He can take away their candlestick. This candlestick represents the light that cannot be hid, except by sin. Christians who lose their candlestick become completely indistinct from those who live around them.

These people hated the Nicolaitans, people who believed in antinomianism. There is a tendency towards lawlessness today. People don't like to be governed and we proclaim the joys of breaking the law and following our own desires. This spirit also resided in the church; many Christians wish to impose their own authority upon the authority of the Scriptures. It seems as though we like to criticise the Bible with a pen knife today. We cut out the parts we don't like and stick with the rest.

Any person who reads or listens to this message is encouraged to hear it. We need to examine ourselves and determine if we have left our fist love. If we have left our first love then we must return to our first love or we are in danger of losing that which makes us distinct in the world.

Those who hear and return to their first love will fully appreciate the fruit of the life that comes from wholehearted devotion and first love.

This church describes the first stage of decay from the pure and vital apostolic church. These Christians are patiently enduring, they are resisting evil men but something is wrong; they have abandoned their first love. There is no longer a passionate devotion to the Lord; discipline has gone from the church.

Christians now argue about points of authority and order. They discuss their traditions and the wisdom of the elders, now authority is vested in men beyond that of the Scriptures.

One of the early principles followed by the children of Israel was to perform their rituals carefully and precisely so that their children would ask 'why do you do these things?" The parents, in reply, were to tell their children all about the Lord who took them from bondage and brought them to the Land flowing with milk and honey.

Christians, like the children of Israel, have been delivered from bondage and set free to serve the Lord. Because we are free we are now able to serve the Lord. We serve the Lord, however, because we love him not because we have to impress him.

We can take great comfort from His love; we love Him because He first loved us. We are not called to obey some demanding tyrant we are called to obey the One who loves us and controls all things. His promises are not dependent on the whim of another, surely we can be confident in His love.

Each Christian needs to examine his or her heart and mind and determine his or her level of discipline. Do we rejoice in our freedom to do certain things or do we rejoice in his love and our freedom to obey him?

You Will Receive Power

"but you will receive power when the Holy Spirit has come upon you; and you shall be My witnesses both in Jerusalem, and in all Judea and Samaria, and even to the remotest part of the earth."

Acts 1:8

One of the most interesting words in our language is the word 'can'. This word is interesting when it is used in the context 'I know I can' or 'I can do it'.

The equivalent work in Greek; meaning 'to be able' is used even more. It is the word 'dunamai'; 'I am able' Associated with this word is another word 'dunamis' meaning 'power'. Our word dynamite is derived from this word.

The interesting thing here is that we can do things because we have power. This power can even be explosive, blasting away all resistance. Scientists know that power is the rate of doing work and work occurs when a force moves something.

Power is important for Christians because with power we can do work and with power we can move away the mountains that seem to defeat us so often. With power we are able to do all things.

Christians can always find real and wonderful power. The best description of the source of that power is found in Acts 1: 8.

If we examine the context o we will have a broader understanding of this verse. The Lord Jesus had been crucified and then rose again in power. He had been with His disciples for some time and they had all seen and worshipped him in His resurrection glory. The Lord Jesus is now ready to go away but the disciples are still asking some question. They want to know about the return to the days of the kingdom. The prophets promised this kingdom.

The Lord carefully and lovingly explains to His disciples that there are some things that they really have no need to know. He tells them that , in spite of this fact, there is something that they really need to know about. For every Christian there is a source of power that is readily available. This is very important because we all need to have power to live our daily lives for God. This benefit is ours to have and we cannot really have power unless we know about this.

There are no conditions to having this power other than the coming of the Holy Spirit. The Lord already told His disciples about the coming of another Comforter. This Comforter was to come and be with them when the Lord Jesus went away. The Holy Spirit is this other Comforter. He will be with the servants of the Lord and comfort, sustain and teach us just as the Lord himself had done. This other Comforter is the Person who will bring us the power that we need.

As the Holy Spirit comes upon us we begin to show evidence of this power. Our Christian lives begin to be vigorous and vital when the Holy Spirit is in control of our lives. The Holy Spirit becomes evident in everything that we do. In an earlier chapter we saw how the leaders of the Jews could tell that Peter and John had been with Jesus. The lives of Christians will show that we have been with the Lord Jesus if the Holy Spirit fills and controls our lives. This power will not only show in our lives but the Holy Spirit also reminds us of all the good things that we have.

Christians who are filled with the Holy Spirit become witnesses to the fact that the Lord Jesus has risen from the dead, forever defeating Satan's power. We are witnesses wherever we are and wherever we go.

Peter and John were unable to contain themselves; they had to speak about the things that they had seen and heard. These men were truly convinced that they were much better off now than they had been before. They had seen and heard the Risen Lord; this even was so remarkable that they could not stop themselves from telling people about this resurrection.

The Holy Spirit continually reminds us of the glory of the Risen Lord Jesus and the joy of knowing that God did not spare His own Son but gave him up for us all.

The Christian life is the greatest life a person can live. We have God's power in us; we are completely free from the anxiety of being responsible for making something of our lives. He has chosen us to be His own and give us the power we need to be His own.

As Christians we can grieve the Holy Spirit[17] by losing our first love for the saints; we can quench the Holy Spirit[18] by complaining and denying His absolute love.

We must make an effort in our lives to obey God in all things even though we may not think that a certain course of action is very good. We must carefully guard that power that has been given to us by using and following the guidance of the Holy Spirit. Let us seek to have the full and abundant life that is ours by the Holy Spirit. We must be obedient to Him in all things.

Did you enjoy reading A Man Under Authority? If you did and you want to read other books by Doug McNaught you can visit www.booksthataregood.com/Christian to find more books like A Man Under Authority.

---

[17] Ephesians 4: 30
[18] 1 Thessalonians 5: 19

www.ingramcontent.com/pod-product-compliance
Ingram Content Group UK Ltd.
Pitfield, Milton Keynes, MK11 3LW, UK
UKHW012247240726
13966UKWH00004B/1339

9 781409 204725